244

Date Due

PSALMS OF MY LIFE

Joseph Bayly

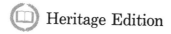 Heritage Edition

Published by
Tyndale House Publishers
Wheaton, Illinois

Coverdale House Publishers Ltd.
London and Eastbourne

Distributed in Canada by
Home Evangel Books Ltd., Toronto, Ontario

Second printing, 1969

Library of Congress Card Catalog No. 72-75243

Copyright © 1969 by Tyndale House Publishers
Wheaton, Illinois

Printed in U.S.A.

1

Lord
my heart fears.
I know that You have said
Fear not
but my heart fears.
Thoughts flash
across the track of my mind
thoughts of evil
not good
loss
not gain
suffering
not joy.
My thoughts are out of control.
They exhume the past
bury the future
make the present
a heavy heavy burden.
Lord
I cannot control
these fears these thoughts.
I cannot look at the future
with peace.
But I trust You.
These fears run wild
careering thoughts of evil
may make it seem
that I don't
but I do.

I trust You Lord.
I know Your thoughts toward me
are of good
not evil.
I fear evil
not You.
Yet fearing wild
I know that even evil
from Your hand
is purest good.
I fear
I trust.
I trust You Lord
I trust Your wisdom
life spanning
Your love
death taming.
I trust You
to know the end of this long beginning mom

2

A Psalm of faith

Thunder
crashing roaring
wakens me.
I get up
to close the window
against the rain.
Lightning tears the sky
for fragmentary moment
I see the yard
wheelbarrow
trees road field
and distant hill.
All is dark again
I return to sleep.
Thank You for the storm
that wakens me
and lightning flash
illumining
things near and far
in usual dark.

3

A Psalm in a Colorado meadow

Twenty wildflowers Lord
no twenty-two.
Here they are
all round where I sit
waiting.
I don't know their names
except arbutus
trailing arbutus
and daisies.
Maybe I could give names
to the rest.
Blue glory in the morning
or blue funk
yellow elf
Aunt Elizabeth's prayerbook
Job's tears
there are a lot of them Lord
all over the meadow.

Lonely gumdrop
the purple kind
that's left in the dish
when all the rest are gone.
Mouse corsage
gopher's hay.
Pink pumps or pinkelumps
Sergeant Pepper's epaulets
Eleanor Rigby's shroud.
Let's see
did I name that one
or those?
I've lost track.
The rest will be nameless
because here come the children
running through the stream
back from climbing
their stone mountain.
Thank You for wild flowers
Lord
mountains
rushing streams
children
each different.
Thank You.

4

A Psalm of love

Thank you for children
brought into being
because we loved.
God of love
keep us loving
so that they
may grow up whole
in love's overflow.

5

A Psalm while packing books

This cardboard box
Lord
see it says
Bursting limit
200 lbs. per square inch.
The box maker knew
how much strain
the box would take
what weight
would crush it.
You are wiser
than the box maker
Maker of my spirit
my mind
my body.
Does the box know
when pressure increases close to
the limit?
No
it knows nothing.
But I know
when my breaking point
is near.
And so I pray
Maker of my soul
Determiner of the pressure
within
upon
me

Stop it
lest I be broken
or else
change the pressure rating
of this fragile container
of Your grace
so that I may bear more.

6

See that speck
Lord
we put it there.
Not really us
Lord
the Russians did.
It shines so bright
as it passes
over Memorial Field
through darkling sky.
It is our evensong.
Whose sun does it reflect?
Why Yours
Lord.
Sputnik
is ours
the sun belongs to You.

7

Let me build a church
Lord
That's big enough for You.
Not big enough for them
or him or her
or me
but You.
Red door
open wide
high walls
enough to hem us in
to You
Your mind
windows without glass
through which
dove may fly
steeple
rising rising
through low clouds
to sky
and star beyond
tolling death
pealing life.

8

High above the clouds
six miles over earth
I think of Time
and Life
not timeless life
of coffee tea or milk
not living water
bread of life
of landing
on hard concrete strip
not flying on
to meet You.
I guess I fear that.
Earthbound in the heavens
Lord
not heavenbound.
Lord have mercy.

9

A Psalm of meaning exchange

I will praise the Lord
for communications media.
For printed page
that says a hundred thousand times
God loves you.
Here's the answer
to your problem
question doubt need.
For radio broadcast
television program
that enters in
where doors are closed
blinds drawn
homes without number
cars
hospital wards
prison cells
barracks
dormitory rooms
and says
You're not alone.
God loves you.

He'll meet you here
and now.
You needn't go out
to strange church
crowded meeting hall.
For records tapes
Braille books
that tell the blind
God loves you.
I will praise the Lord
for communications media.
I will praise the Lord
for a man
a woman
who grasps trembling hand
under oxygen tent
who sits on edge
of barracks bed
who looks the prisoner
in the eye
who buys a Coke for student
who walks with blind
and says
God loves you
and they know
He does
too.

10

Tonight
Lord Jesus Christ
You sat at supper
with Your friends.
It was a simple meal
that final one
of lamb
unleavened bread
and wine.
Afterward
You went out to die.
How many other meals You shared
beside the lake
fried fish and toasted bread
at Simon's banquet hall a feast
at Lazarus' home in Bethany
the meal that Martha cooked
on mountain slope
where You fed hungry crowd
at close of tiring day.
Please sit with us tonight
at our small meal
of soup and rolls and tea.
Then go with us
to feast of bread and wine
that You provide
because afterward
You went out to die.

11

A Psalm at Children's Hospital

I find it hard Lord
agonizing hard
to stand here
looking through the glass
at this my infant son.
What suffering
is in this world
to go through pain of birth
and then through
pain of knife
within the day.
What suffering
is in the world
this never ending
pain parade
from birth
to death.
He moves
a bit
not much
how could an infant
stuffed with tubes
cut sewed and bandaged
move more than that?

Some day he'll shout
and run a race
roll down a grassy hill
ice skate
on frosty night like this.
He'll sing
and laugh
I know he will Lord.
But if not
if You should take him home
to Your home
help me then remember
how Your Son suffered
and You stood by
watching
agonizing watching
waiting
to bring all suffering to an end
forever
on a day
yet to be.
Look Lord
he sleeps.
I must go now.
Thank You for staying
nearer than oxygen
than dripping plasma
to my son.
Please be that near
to mother
sister brothers
and to me.

12

A Psalm of St. Elmo, Colorado

This ghost town
Lord
once live
now dead
boarded up
against the world
the flesh
the devil.
The devil? No
he lives here
in shuttered house
abandoned mine
boarded post office
tavern store.
He's at home
in ghost town
not town alive
with children
hammers
violins.

He wanders
in a solitary place.
This cemetery
Lord
graves marked
with weathered boards
and stones
and picket fence
does he live here
in ghost town graveyard
place of the doubly dead?
No I live here.
My angels guard
the graves
of those I know
in ghost town.
They are the living ones.

13

This is the day
the Lord has made.
The Lord?
Today?
Yesterday perhaps
could claim Your craft
or hopefully tomorrow
but not today
this disappointing day so filled
with problems
needs
despair and doubt.
This is the day
the Lord has made
and making it
He'll give the strength
and hope
to take me through.
This is the day
the Lord has made
so I'll be glad
and I'll rejoice in it.

14

A Psalm of praise for the tribes

I will sing
of the tribes of earth
who have turned
from darkness
to light
not flickering dying campfire
but sun of opening day.
Walamo
Kambatta Hadiya
Yoruba
Mixtec Tzeltal Cakchiquel
Shapras Aucas
Lisu Katu
Picts
Angles Saxons Swabians
Visigoths.
I will sing
of men and women
who brought light
to the tribes.
Ohman Bergsten
Crouch
Pike Slocum Townsend
Cox and Anderson

The five who died
Elliot Saint
Fraser
Smith
Boniface Willibrand
Ulfilas.
I will sing
of the Light
of earth's tribes
who will shine in them
forever.

15

A Psalm when things are going well

Save me
God
from success.
I fear it
more than failure
which alerts me
to my nature
limitations
destiny.
I know that
any success
apart from Your Spirit
is mere euphemism
for failure.

16

I'm alone Lord
alone
a thousand miles from home.
There's no one here who knows my name
except the clerk
and he spelled it wrong
no one to eat dinner with
laugh at my jokes
listen to my gripes
be happy with me about what happened today
and say that's great.
No one cares.
There's just this lousy bed
and slush in street outside
between the buildings.
I feel sorry for myself
and I've plenty of reason
to.
Maybe I ought to say
I'm on top of it
praise the Lord
things are great
but they're not.
Tonight
it's all
gray slush.

17

Thank You for music
Lord
Handel and Haydn Society
and Boston Symphony
present
Handel's Messiah.
He shall feed His flock
like a shepherd
shall gather the lambs with His arm
and carry them in His bosom.
Students on Fairview Island
singing
Who is on the Lord's side
who will serve the King?
Mother holding little boy
rocking
humming
all through the night
my Savior will be watching
and like a river glorious
is God's perfect peace.
Little group of people
before an open grave
singing
Jesus I love Thee
and up from the grave He arose.

18

I take this step
Lord
in faith.
Faith that You
have confronted me
with this opening
Faith that You
have led me to accept
Faith that this change
will be a means
to greater holiness
and love
to You
for me
my wife
our children
Faith
that You will make me
able for this new work
so that I may add
in every way
to what You
are already doing
where I go

Faith
that You will care
for mother sister
friends needy ones
we leave behind
Faith that You will make me
creative in my work
and in the exercise
of other gifts
Faith that by this change
You will make
life and self we share
my wife's and mine
and ours together
more real
more full
than it has been to now
Faith that this change
will bring much blessing
to each of our children
Faith in Your promise
that when You put forth
Your own sheep
You go before them.
Lord I will not go
unless You do this.

19

This pew
is soft
cushioned.
Thank You Lord
for our new sanctuary
acoustically
near perfect
so we can hear
no matter how deaf
lighting
by an illumination engineer
so we can see
with even dimmest sight
air conditioned
so we can shut out
the heat
be cool
no matter what.
It's a great new sanctuary
This soft pew
cushions me
against the wood.

20

A Psalm for Christmas Eve

Praise God for Christmas.
Praise Him for the Incarnation
for the Word made flesh.
I will not sing
of shepherds watching flocks
on frosty night
or angel choristers.
I will not sing
of stable bare in Bethlehem
or lowing oxen
wise men
trailing distant star
with gold and frankincense and myrrh.
Tonight I will sing
praise to the Father
who stood on heaven's threshold
and said farewell to His Son
as He stepped across the stars
to Bethlehem
and Jerusalem.
And I will sing
praise to the infinite eternal Son
who became most finite
a Baby
who would one day be executed
for my crimes.
Praise Him in the heavens.
Praise Him in the stable.
Praise Him in my heart.

21

Praise the Lord.
Praise Him in the Rockies
riding mountain trails.
Praise Him
beside tumbling
rushing
rocky
white capped stream.
Praise Him
in high meadow
still forest.
Praise Him on the Cape
eating lobster, clams
walking rainswept beach
barefoot.
Praise Him on Mount Baker
holding ski rope
going uphill
then down.
Praise Him in the snowfall.
Praise Him in the lodge
sitting by the fire
looking out at stars.
Praise Him at the desk
phoning
writing
meeting
planning.

Praise Him in high places
and in low
in excitement
and monotony.
I will sing to the Lord
as long as I live.
I will be glad in the Lord
in the Lord.

22

A Psalm of praise

Thank You God
that You see
armies march
a sparrow fall
hear
atom's blast
a baby's cry
smell
volcano's flow
a man's sweat
feel
contour of mountains
a little lump
taste
ocean's salt
my tears.

23

I plead guilty
Lord
I stand awaiting
sentence
my crimes
spread out before You
Just Judge
of all the earth
I have no words
to lessen guilt.
No other can I blame
distant Adam
near people
except myself.
My guilt I bear
alone.
Alone?
Another stood alone
before You
and took my sentence
Lord.
Now I am free
to praise you
Just Judge
to please You
Criminal in my place.

24

What waste Lord
this ointment precious
here outpoured
is treasure great
beyond my mind to think.
For years
until this midnight
it was safe
contained
awaiting careful use
now broken
wasted
lost.
The world is poor
so poor it needs each drop
of such a store.
This treasure spent
might feed a multitude
for all their days
and then yield more.
This world is poor?
It's poorer now
the treasure's lost.
I breathe its lingering fragrance
soon even that
will cease.
What purpose served?

The act is void of reason
sense
Lord
madmen do such deeds
not sane.
The sane man hoards his treasure
spends with care
if good
to feed the poor
or else to feed himself.
Let me alone Lord
You've taken from me
what I'd give Your world.
I cannot see
such waste
that You should take
what poor men need.
You have a heaven
full of treasure
could You not wait
to exercise Your claim
on this?
O spare me Lord forgive
that I may see
beyond this world
beyond myself
Your sovereign plan
or seeing not
may trust You
Spoiler of my treasure.
Have mercy Lord
here is my quitclaim.

25

How happy are those
who take the Gospel
to other lands.
They obey Your command
Lord Jesus
Your command to tell
the Good News
everywhere
to every person
in the whole world.
They forsake
kindred and friends
houses and land
comfort security things
to go tell
teach
heal
love.
They are the great ones
of this generation
of whom the world
is not worthy.
They are the ones
whom the world pities.
Poor world.
Poor pitiful world.

They are Your ambassadors
sent by You
to declare an end
to hostility
and announce peace
through Your death
and endless life.
How happy are those
who take the Gospel
to other lands.

26

A Psalm of anticipation

Lord Christ
Your servant
Martin Luther
said he only had
two days
on his calendar
today
and that day
and that's
what I want too.
And I want
to live
today
for
that day.

27

A Psalm of the fat camel

This needle's eye
Lord
it is so very small
and I'm so very big
I can't squeeze through
not even little finger.
But then
I'm part of
the affluent society.
We've shown
as never people did before
how to get
acquire
build up
squander
and still get more
more things
cars houses
land rosebushes
money
stocks and bonds
more gross national product
and more defenses of it all
more of everything
this side of
needle's eye.
Lord have mercy.
Do a necessary miracle.

28

A Psalm in Mojave Desert

I said
this desert land is barren
void of life and beauty.
I drive for miles
see nothing
only sand and sage
feel nothing
only wind and heat
taste nothing
but spit dried spit.
He said
have you ever driven
in spring
through this same desert
seen blossoms flower
gorgeous wild?
It's all a thing of timing.
Seeds of beauty
are there now hidden
waiting fall of rain
to bring them life.
Lord send rain
upon my world
my life
I'm tired of dried spit.

29

A Psalm about the shortness of life

I said
O Lord
let me end the work
You gave to me to do.
So much
must yet be done
before the dark
so little time
remains
before I'm home.
You are eternal
God
a thousand years to You
is but a passing day.
You scatter ages
I hoard my hours.
Please understand
my need for time
to do Your will
complete my job.
I understand
He said
I do
I only had
three years
of days
and I was through.

30

A Psalm requesting faith

Give me courage Lord
to take risks
not the usual ones
respected
necessary
relatively safe
but those I could avoid
the go for broke ones.
I need courage
not just because
I may fall on my face
or worse
but others seeing me
a sorry spectacle
if it should happen
will say
he didn't know what he was doing
or he's foolhardy
or he's old enough to know
you lead from the side
instead of letting yourself be caught
in wild stampede.
Give me courage Lord
to take unnecessary risks
live at tension
instead of opting out.
Give me the guts to put up
instead of shutting up.

When it comes right down to it
Lord
I choose to be Your failure
before anyone else's success.
Keep me from reneging
on my choice.

31

A Psalm of personal need

Lord, my heart is a ghetto
walled off
dark
depressed
danger filled
hurting.
Move in, Lord.
Renew it
renew my heart
destroy, burn
raze
remove.
Build it fresh
and then You live there.
You Lord.
Because then
it'll stay
clean
pure
new.

32

Thank You for our leaders
for pastors
who feed us
serve us and our children
as Your ministers
Son of God
who came not to be served
but to serve
for theologians
who give us answers
questions
reasons for our hope
from Your Word
Father of Lights
for evangelists
who harvest the field
You have brought
to fruition
Holy Spirit
for teachers
who make us think
of You
ourselves and others
because You have taught them.
Thank You for our leaders
Your followers.

33

A Psalm of extremity

I cry tears
to you Lord
tears
because I cannot speak.
Words are lost
among my fears
pain
sorrows
losses
hurts
but tears
You understand
my wordless prayer
You hear.
Lord
wipe away my tears
all tears
not in distant day
but now
here.

34

Two days ago
You made the universe
earth sun moon stars
and everything
including man
praise God.
Yesterday
You lived among us
shared our life
taught healed and loved
died for our sins
rose from the dead
praise God.
Today You live in us
who own You Lord
praise God.
Tomorrow You'll return
to claim Your universe
and rule
and every knee
in heaven and earth and under earth
shall bow
and every tongue confess
that You
are Lord
praise God.

35

A Psalm of wandering

Lord You know
I'm such a stupid sheep.
I worry
about all sorts of things
whether I'll find grazing land
still cool water
a fold at night
in which I can feel safe.
I don't.
I only find troubles
want
loss.
I turn aside from You
to plan my rebel way.
I go astray.
I follow other shepherds
even other stupid sheep.
Then when I end up
on some dark mountain
cliffs before
wild animals behind
I start to bleat
Shepherd Shepherd
find me save me
or I die.
And You do.

36

You made known Your ways
to Moses
God
Your acts
to his people Israel.
They only saw
the sea divide
and swallow Pharaoh's host
the fire by night
the cloud by day.
They tasted manna
quail
drank water from the rock.
It was enough
for them to live
by what You did
leave reason to another.
Not Moses
he was a different sort
who prayed
Show me now
Your ways O God.
And You did.
You let him see
the principles
behind Your acts
and past the principles

the character displayed
eternal character
that forms the principles
the acts
and all.
Make me a Moses
God
dissatisfied with anything
short of You.

37

A Psalm of poverty

Lord Christ
You loved the poor.
It was a sign
that You were who
You claimed to be.
You bothered
with them
preached to them
invited to be rich and full.
Forgive me Lord
for falling short
of such a love as Yours
that broke through crust
of our poverty
for a beggar
like me.

38

In times of crisis
Lord
when we don't know
which way
the scales will tip
all else is
unimportant.
We couldn't care less about money
things
about what we eat
or whether.
We don't notice
rebuffs
comments that would ordinarily
disturb us.
Our mind is honed
to single edge.
You loom
above all else
fill our horizon.
Your will
becomes our food
our drink
the very air we breathe.
Too soon
the crisis passes

and we're right back
where we were
before.
Dear Lord forgive.

39

A Psalm of dignity

Thank You
Lord Christ
for treating every other person
as an end
not a means
including me.
Thank You
that You never climbed
on other person's shoulders
never used a man or woman
boy or girl
as if he were a thing.
Thank You
for refusing to invade
the freedom
You have given us.
Thank You for refusing
to manipulate us
pressure us
maneuver us into a corner.
Thank You for treating us
as if we shared Your image.

40

Lord of reality
make me real
not plastic
synthetic
pretend phony
an actor playing out his part
hypocrite.
I don't want
to keep a prayer list
but to pray
nor agonize to find Your will
but to obey
what I already know
to argue
theories of inspiration
but submit to Your Word.
I don't want
to explain the difference
between eros and philos
and agape
but to love.
I don't want
to sing as if I mean it
I want to mean it.
I don't want
to tell it like it is
but to be it
like You want it.

I don't want
to think another needs me
but I need Him
else I'm not complete.
I don't want
to tell others how to do it
but to do it
to have to be always right
but admit it
when I'm wrong.
I don't want
to be a census taker
but an obstetrician
nor an involved person
a professional
but a friend.
I don't want
to be insensitive
but to hurt
where other people hurt
nor to say
I know how you feel
but to say God knows
and I'll try
if you'll be patient with me
and meanwhile I'll be quiet.
I don't want
to scorn the clichés
of others
but to mean everything I say
including this.

41

Let's celebrate Easter
with the rite
of laughter.
Christ died and rose
and lives.
Laugh like a woman
who holds her first baby.
Our enemy death
will soon be destroyed.
Laugh like a man
who finds he doesn't have cancer
or he does but now there's a cure.
Christ opened wide
the door of heaven.
Laugh like children
at Disneyland's gates.
This world is owned by God
and He'll return to rule.
Laugh like a man
who walks away uninjured
from a wreck
in which his car was totaled.
Laugh
as if all the people in the whole world
were invited to a picnic
and then invite them.